I0410491

Thunder Road

By

Sont

© 2003 by Sont. All rights reserved.

No part of this book may be reproduced, stored in a retrieval
system, or transmitted by any means, electronic,
mechanical, photocopying, recording, or otherwise, without
written permission from the author.

ISBN: 1-4033-9196-3 (e-book)
ISBN: 1-4033-9197-1 (Paperback)

Library of Congress Control Number: 2002095537

This book is printed on acid free paper.

Printed in the United States of America
Bloomington, IN

1stBooks – rev. 03/04/03

For Oletha and Carolyn,
Gloria and Paula,
and B.J.

ACKNOWLEDGMENTS

Acknowledgment is made to the following journals and anthologies for poems, or earlier versions of poems, published in them: *Anthology of New American Poets* ("Helen of McElroy's"), *Galaxy of Verse* ("1-2-3/1-2-3"; "Falling for Poetry"), *Once Upon a Poet* ("When Wings Deceive"), *Southern Review* ("Between Touches"), *Southwest Review* ("The Black and White of It"), *Tendril* ("Clandestine Touches"), *Understanding* ("U-Turn: To Nonconformity").

The Author thanks Doubleday and Company, Inc. for permission to use a quote from *The Collected Poems of Theodore Roethke*, 1954 in the poem entitled "Had He Been Taught: Turn and Counter-turn." Also, the Harold Matson Company, Inc., for permission to quote from *The Ruined Cottage*, ed. Jonathan Wordsworth, 1968, in the poem "Materialism: Too Much With Us Late and Soon."

The Author wishes to thank Mr. and Mrs. Kenneth R. Jamison for their love and support, Terry Reed Jamison Glover for her constant influence, Kenneth Damon Jamison for his encouragement, Marie Harrott for enthusiasm over her work, Deborah E. Morris for her invaluable help in preparing the manuscript, Gary L. Tyler for sharing the dream, and Oletha Givens for being everything a friend should be. The Author is also incomprehensively grateful to her husband, Charles E. Tyler, for his suggestions, love and patience between touches.

CONTENTS

SCENIC ROUTE

DETOURS

CITY LIMITS

PEDESTRIAN CROSSING

DEAD-END: NO OUTLET

POET'S COVE

SCENIC ROUTE

Sont

Thunder Road

On Thunder Road
I lost my virginity,
but there no thunder was heard.

Of what is there to tell?
Truth? Rumors:
Fact, fiction—so much lies between

…magic unfolds from a black-top hat
that is night, two hundred years
of little white lies (told to girls
to keep them "nice') fly…

Iniquitous…inviting—
the kind of place every hometown
knows, Thunder Road zigs
over the land to lick
at the mouth of the lake;
a snake, a great serpent of old:
drawing lovers to neck, to play, to rumors
make and find-out all.

Rumor has it: when the right two
"make-it'—thunder rumbles,
a storm follows,
rains pelt-out metrical rhythms
of a strength and beat
of hearts in cars.

Tough one to follow?
Greek mythology's got nothing
On the stories mom and grandmas told:

a piece… "You have to do IT even if you
don't want to," …another… "I never
let a man touch me there in my life—not
even your grandfather!" …weave in…a flannel
nightgown, a curse if a man sees what's
under it…paint a picture…a white dress
moving toward a faceless man…you have
an idea of what I knew.

Not very much.

But that didn't stop me.
I wanted to know of Thunder Road.

Like a birthmark,
unsightly or not, blotched or beautified,
the memory is something a girl never loses…

I smell rain;
I remember…

     …he is a tree over the road,
on me a shadow—limbs, leaf-fringed,
hover over us. Enticed by their sway,
I reach for them, pull them down
to block pain flowing forth
like wax from a candle—hot, burning,

instantly hardening soft, enveloping
what it has touched, making it
numb—bursts womanhood—not of blossom—but
of something withered like the ground
below on Thunder Road.

I break from the encasement,
the entanglement.
Free and nestled like a bird in that tree
outside the car, I imagine looking down
on girls all over the world
who are just like me:

a scarfed girl of Hamadan's Land
shakes as she lowers veil, enters
the hall of womanhood half-cocked; in a land
of black forests, a *fraulein* blinks at some
Hans; a girl of Crete, before a mirror,
practices wiles; a Russian gymnast bites
her lip and wonders if it will enlarge
her breasts; a Spanish senorita saves
face by keeping a certain place from
being touched while her chaperon
looks away; a Libyan lovely looks
downcast because she must keep
her place and wait; all like me…

　　　　…the leaf
of some limp flower falls,
brushes against me;

I listen and am surrounded by silence
and the swaying of some unseasoned tree
on Thunder Road.

I hear nothing.
I feel nothing—except…a shadow move
and a drop of dew that is sweat,
not of mine, I can't even taste the salt
of sweat on my own lips.

After that, for almost a year…

…I walked the house like a timid mouse
whose entrance to its store of hordes
had been blocked.

How could they do it—Mom, Grandma—when
it was so little fun, so much pain?
Not a bit like the fresh rain of rumors.

      I was a rocket—
powerful, ready—next time,
I wasn't going to be left
on the ground or have my head
stuck there or up—anywhere.

I started a countdown: read books,
talked to some friends, then on ten
and counting-down…I met him.

He listened; he knew
what to say and do: "Weather," he said,
"…doesn't at all matter—in sunshine
or under stars at night,
in times of war or winter…where you
are…doesn't matter—when you're in love,
it will be good…let me take you
to Thunder Road."

On Thunder Road
he taught me to love—
like children learn the alphabet,
one-letter-at-a-time until I could
sing to him words.

I heard thunder
as he kissed away,
with well-fueled lips,
all of those old rumors and myths.

I stared with him at clear skies
and he held me until it rained.

1969

It was more than just a year,
more than freedom of sex
or a search for sanctuary,

more than was told of in
smoke or held in long, easy
breaths called tokes.

Acerbic exclamations laid
seed in long hair and words
most feared were allotment,

apportionment, draft and
quotes like "Do you share?"
Giving of ourselves like whores

we offered amnesty among ourselves,
burned bras and cards and sang
of men and war, but beat no drums—

marched blue-jeaned and flag donned.
Anarchism fed the air. Fools
called it apathy and stared.

Standing in lines of protest
and despair, we got our shadows
back; America buried soldiers

in magazine stacks. It was
more than a year, nearly twenty
years ago that we, a nation,

collided with our soul.

At the Best Universities

They come. Some with
Something; none with
Nothing. All to get
The everything.

Like hunters for prey
They stalk quarry
In every word professors
Say. They are silent.

Instincts crouch in
Them and spring forth
On days of exams. They
Feed on grades.

Their prowess is
Procrastination juggled
On demand. They fear
Only static on MTV.

Silent, salient—
Something is growing
Here between the battles
And the beer. Something

Is surfacing. When all
Is quiet on the front:

We listen for the roar
Or the thump.

Breezes Before the Blow

It leaves us
hanging:

the light touch,

it is never
quite enough.

Effervescent.

The lighter
the touch
the closer we move
like an itch
to finger's reach.

The light touch,

a teaser,
sure enough:

a taunting temptress
balancing bait
before the play
in full
that …

keeps us playing.

Clandestine Touches

Speechlessly,
I can listen
to your silence
all...day.

I can watch
nothing
seeing the everything
playing in your eyes:

moving in motions
to and fro;

hiding truths
and private lies.

This is the
everyday game
we play:

Hide-and-Seek.

(You hide and I
try to peek.)

Chinese Puzzle

When I floundered
for the pieces,
you placed them
within my
reach.

Together
we created
an inseparable
peace where ridges
lie unseen,
where corners
turn into streets
of dreams producing
matted enigma
of you and me
that Confucius
could not help
but see.

Between Touches

As everything else
in my life has been,
our togetherness has
fallen somewhere be/
tween pleasure and sin.

It was as if we were meant
to be (somewhere between
now and eternity) thrown
together to be slung apart.

For as every sleeping child
will wake be he blessed
to boast another day; as fast
as pages in a teen magazine
are fanned; as quickly as
our youthful wishes
of yet another year turn
gray more speedily than
tint can tame—
we all go our separate
ways, but with us go
the moments time
can never touch: the
      saffronic smiles traipsing
      across associations; the distant
      acknowledgments we'll independently
      make while crossing one another
      shopping (concert/café/movie or lake)
      passing by with highway "Hi's" that
      touch a familiar face and fill space.

Sont

Who knows what directions our fate?
We do not know what course our lives
will take; we only know of the present
and of it must our memories make;
for in the end, we won't remember
what was said to cause laughter;
we won't remember lies shed,
nor the reconciliations after.

In retrospect there will
only be you and I,
remembering, in space
that time controls
between touches.

DETOURS

Sont

Detour

It's not that I can't
let go of yesterday;
it's that I can't
hold on to today;

And it seems that stagger I
to the shoulder's forbidden zone,
between the white lines,
and see other's forgotten bones.

Move we like the Pale Horse
and his rider, algetic and doomed,
destined to forgo rest or sleep
or dare cry the moon.

I could stand all this irrelevance
were this a path to any reality
or the journey made but any sense
from sketched to etched in memory.

U-Turn To Nonconformity

I dream my friends and I are
Floating like helium balloons.
Then, without a pop,

the air is gone and I
am struggling to breathe
and kicking my feet.

It is dark and deep;
frightening things flit by
as feathers against a tree's trunk

that is me: sinking into the depths
of something (not air, not water)
that is heavy, empty and alone.

Beware: Falling Rocks

Do not laugh; do not smile:
if you but show an ounce
of emotion,

I'll drown in mine now
held at bay
like the desert

from the nearest ocean.
This is one of those
awesome times

when the heart,
if it but hears a
quake as it

yearns for the
silence of
sympathy.

will—without a whisper—break.

Yield: Crab Crossing

There is probably no animal
in the world that suffers
the temptation that we
do to look backwards.

Thinking of what we should
have done, of what we could
have, or of simply doing what
we didn't—that is our lot.

That's us, the superior
breed: the ones with the
cricks in their necks.

I don't know how many times
I've heard, "If I knew then
what I know now!"… What?

Would you be any younger
than you were then? Would
you be any prettier than you
were or even think you were?
Would you be richer?
Healthier?

You'd surely have a stiff
neck from looking straight
ahead. After all, isn't that
exactly what we humans
are all about:

wanting what we can't have
and crawling around sidewise
over what we do?

It is our nature to dig in sand.
It is our nature to live and ad-lib.

In Love, But Not Falling

I won't lie. It's
not the brightest
day I've seen,
and though some
distant birds
are calling, the
only one I see is
a melancholy one
that seems to be
looking around for
something that fell
out of its nest.

            Okay—
So I'm not the romantic.
Does that make you love
me less? If you want me
to, I'll read for you:
maybe some Browning—
Elizabeth, that is,
not a monologue from
her old man.
Of course, I can
make you feel
that with you
in love I am
falling; but if I
do that, I'll never
let you know me.

To the furthest
mountain top with
you I will go, but
to the deepest ocean?
No.

The Answer is No Ode

What happened to our timing?

Do you remember when clocks
were like freckles obliterated
into a tan by a sun overhead
that was our love melting
moments and skin.

Remember when we said we
should buy one pair of shoes
because our ever-plodding
practiced feet walked so
close together to be yet
so unfettered?

Do you remember when I
exhaled and you said
you did breathe?

Where is that oasis we
made where we did once
run to one another and
drink?

My rhetorician,
is this how love dies;
with questions that have
no answers and with Why's?

We Learn By Our Mistakes—Or Riots

I cringed and shut my eyes
to unbearable scenes as
portrayed the tube,
electrically, some
of life's cruelties.

The fiction made me cry
and the tears salted
my mind with questions
of "How could they?"
and "Why?" and on my
but—I looked on with
indigestion and a sigh.

Somewhere in the darkness
at my side, my roommate
cleared her throat as if
to dislodge me, the lump,
from it and she spoke
with not an ounce of pride.

"And you are not even Black;"
not as accusation, but as
matter-of-fact, "Think how
you'd feel knowing that the
movie is not over yet, but somebody
keeps turning on the lights!"

Poor and Proud

Aristocratic and aloof:
what a stupid goose!

You dip your head
only to feed;
don't condescend
to me.

Quack on with your
demands and waddle
over inherited lands.

As you poise feathered
and furred, pass me by
without saying a word.

1-2-3 / 1-2-3
for Jessica

Dance, dance, dance!
Listen to the music
hearts play to dreams.

Leap to possibilities;
leave lull-a-byes to
sleepy-eyes afraid to
open for what might be.

Even if your feet
never leave the ground,
exercise aspirations that
jump and move around
taking you to where
ballads abound in billows
on isolated clouds.

Dance, dance, dance!
It is your time around.

Far, far beneath you
is everything ordinary,
stationary and green.

Dance to the music
hearts play to dreams.

Had He But Been Taught: Turn and Counter-turn

"But who would count eternity in days?
These old bones live to learn her wanton ways:
(I measure time by how a body sways)."
                              —Theodore Roethke

If she had been wood
like some sturdy
oaken door,

he'd have knocked
on her until she
let him in,

but she was glass
so he broke her
just to see

how much he could
pick up without
getting cut.

When he had picked
up just enough, he
made from her an

hourglass: she
told time by the turn
of his hand;

entrapped and momentary,
she was sand for this man.

Sont

CITY LIMITS

Sont

The Pasture Concrete

We're going out to work:
(for salaries…bills)
and of little important
do we think other
than of when you sent
me roses—pink.

We're making days?
by seconds inbetween.

We're going out to earn
Elastic cash: though
Work is not exotic
In the least,
Daydreams squeeze,
Break clocks breathe.

We're making days
By seconds inbetween
in—

the pasture concrete.

Computer _ _ _ _Jargon

Insert this & *log-on*
we're going to *new*
this relationship.

No—I'm not going
      to stay with
      you.

No—you didn't
      program me.

You don't have
the *key.*

Insert this & log-on
we're going to new
this relationship.

No—there's no
      chip on my
      shoulder.

No—I won't be
      processed.

Byte your lip
&
insert this:

the *Data* is not
accessible.

Three Rings of a Circus Dream
(And Inbetween)

Going with a grown man
(who had never been)
to the circus
in the city—

seeing the wonder,
the excitement
in his eyes
vacant in the eyes
of those at his side—

I thought...(more
like made a wish
on balloons floating
to the ceiling like
captured stars)...

How advantageous it
would be to have
the ungrateful experience
poverty (like they did
shows) that they might
learn to appreciate
all of those things
they simply (not even
for granted) take.

B. & B., What a show
on earth that would
be!

Acropolis in Bliss?

The city lives,
but does not dream.
Insomniac—bulimia bound—it
gorges itself on a bit
of every living thing.
                              The
Rumblings of traffic reign
Over echoes from each cement
Hole; indigestion, gut pains,
Gray asphalt and sweat—remind us
That we are all alone.
                              Symphonized
stares, synchronized shouts stalk
isolation, surge on despair;
sincerity and sympathy suffocate
in an atmosphere conducive to
nightmares.
                              The living things—
the traffic, the ticker-tape, the
pounds of work—are the only things
that speak. The dead don't know
hurt.
              The city's ornaments—walked
in—suspend over segmented souls who
look down on those up-and-coming
needles and needs from below.

Teetering between while lines and
neon signs: red, yellow, green
on concrete—twenty-four hours a day,
everyday—the city screams and does
not sleep.

The city lives,
but does not dream.
Is that why it has gone insane?

Materialism: Too Much With Us Late and Soon

"Getting and spending, we lay waste our powers:
Little we see in Nature that is ours…"
                    —William Wordsworth

YARDBIRDS ELECTRICAL SUPPLIES:
I read driving by a sign and
thought, would that I could
buy something that
would light me up inside.

Salaries x per @ # gross;
green on a papernote, pieces
of minutes, hours, days—gone—pressed
into punch-ins and machines:

5's—10's—20's—50's

and luxury laminated in plastic,
obligations extended to who knows when
filling our every need and whim—

leave so much space left in me for hire.

Would that we could buy something
to light us up inside.

Would that we could get
and spend for something
in nature to be ours.

But Wordsworth, the signs—
the signs today just lead
us to buy.

Where the Streets Are Silent

on my street,
the children do not sing

they rap and zap each other
with imaginary things, they yell
like auctioneers and at about the
same pace, but never a song comes
from a single street face.

When i first came to my window
to write, i was surprised: not
by the noise or the violence or
the gossip or the games but
by the silence

the children on my street
do not sing

they play: they curse/they run
they taunt/they scavenge in puddles
throw trash/ say anything/ do anything
dangerous or fun/run the streets
rain or sun/climb (fences/cars/sheds
garages/old boats/construction piles)
each other/but no stars

they laugh: at dogs that bark/at cars
at falls/at the mailman/at broken toys
and even arms/at bad jokes/at limbs too

high to reach/at moms and dads/at cats
at each other for anything
but they do not sing

because i pulled two of them apart,
made them shake hands and tell me how
it started, they slouch towards my
yard like little boxers and their
entourages when conflicts start; my
frown, the referee, means more to them
than Old Lady Conner's constant smile
which they love to try and dissolve as
she skirts them on maneuvers to her box

they are imaginative: they call me
Rooster because i'm here pecking away
At this typewriter all day; one day when
i was cocked outside, i spanked the bottom
of one of them who ran in front of a car,
the runt hugged my knees and soaked them
with a flood only a child can bring to relief

they cry but do not sing

they aren't bad kids: they run to help me
with my groceries since i'm a celebrity
(being the only adult they think doesn't work)
and none of my window get smashed or trash
gashed; i rarely have to mow because they
run the lawn down like little billy-goats
trampling to ground anything they can't eat

i love to watch them play (i think it
is play): they are rough and die hard like
falling rocks, they are MIA's, Rambo, Karate
experts, guerilla fighters and fighter-pilots,
He-men and in a battle they tear clothes

one of the strangest things was a response
i got to a story i told one of them about
Pegasus and how he burned his wings, the boy
said when i was through: "at least he got to soar"

i can't begin to tell the times i've heard
them score on one another metaphorically
relating every detail of the lives they live in
little exquisite quips: they score on faces and
shapes, on eyelashes and mistakes, on walks and
friends' lisps, on family and cars and even one the
clothes hanging on the lines behind their houses

at night when those clothes are dry and the
empty lines link each echo of the day to
screams still bouncing from the silent cement
street, i think about the children behind the walls

and wonder if they are singing

Sont

PEDESTRIAN CROSSING

Sont

The Black and White of It

Magpies are you and I,
Ash and ember, a shadow and a star
Under fluorescent lights;
Inertly, we avert Argus-eyes.

Strange it is that you
Of subtle shade of hue,
One of Nature's rarest jades,
Must endure criticism undue.

Irony it is that I
Find no quiet night in which
To set my song to you on high,
No night in which to shine.

Magpies we are,
You and I,
External opposites,
A shadow and a star.

Helen of McElroy's

Helen, in her worn
houseshoes and her shawl,
shuffles through the
grocery like a bull.

Her horns are replaced
by a cart which she uses
to plow her way through
corridors of food and
cardboard people who point
to her what's good.

                        From
Another aisle I notice
the lines and bulges
beneath her clothes and
cut my eyes when she
catches me staring
at a tear in her hose.
Now,
she holds before her
a coupon and freezes upon
it resembling a grotesque
caricature of the advertising
statuettes. Oh, Lord, I think,
don't let me someday look
like that. And she must
have read my look before she
moved, for as I ducked
and busied myself at the
shelves, she—like a wounded
bull avoiding the cape—
scuttled by my cart.

At the register as
I wait for my turn, I
see Helen, my buxom
cohort make it to her chute,
and I am almost choked to see
that she did, indeed, read
my mind and stands there
now in line with only a
look of—I'll show you—
and a bottle of permanent
hair dye.

When Wings Deceive

Like a beautiful, beveled
butterfly, she flits about
the apartment complex
landing on anything
she can find.

The neighbors call her
Amelia Earcry,
and they told me
when I moved in,
I would soon see why.

Within a week,
I witnessed how witty
and well-placed is
Amelia's nickname:
suitors for her come and go
like scalpers picking up
tickets for a sure sell-out;
there is always a line
of different guys
inspecting our sidewalk
as they scoot to her door.
But the thing that cinches
the creativity of it all
is that each time the sap
runs dry on what the complex
calls: "one of Amelia's bouquets,"
she cries.

Sometimes passers-by
can hear her crying through
her door: crying like I've
never heard a butterfly cry before.

Trying to be not so critical
and a little more cordial,
I stopped to talk to her
today as she stood outside
her door. To my sympathy
and surprise, I quickly
realized that the beautiful
distant butterfly is really
only an ordinary moth.

Vampires of Love

With acrylic nails less
hard than their hearts,
they hold objects of love
to them like hostages
clutched in the dark.

Swaying hips beneath
seductive red lips
beckon lives into a
permanent plastic land
of the living dead:

into worlds of wealth,
of costly eternal beauty,
into transplants, suck-outs
and hypnotizing illusions
of up-lifted youth

run the pretty prey,
the unsuspecting quarry,
the vampire victims,
who learn to suck up
life like water from

goblets of blood red wine
held by hands with long
perfect acrylic nails
less hard than the hearts
of those who own them.

Movie-Goers

They stand in lines
beside silhouettes
which accompany them
steadily toward
the door.

They pay at a
window for the
services to be
rendered within a
dark room where they
will enjoy private
orgasms.

All is legal
and complete—the
perfect fantasy—
anything one can read into a

twenty-by-twenty screen.

Celeb

He yearns for the obscurity
of being ordinary and back
home, but the poverty back
there keeps him alone.

How dreams and words have
for him changed. Sick of
autograph hounds, he now
calls fans "bowwows" and
hovels into hotels and cars
wishing only that his clothes
were armor and he no
chivalrous sort.
     He yearns.
His stomach churns. He longs
for those days when clothes
were old, when he followed
behind his dad and ducked
his head when people stared
at holes in their clothes.

But dreams of bologna wrapped
in fresh white bread, slugged
down by lukewarm cola drown
with the music of the band.

He wants to go back home,
but remember his dad's
old clothes, he grabs an
hors d'oeuvre and skirts out
to clothe himself in song.

Terry

If I had to be
trapped anywhere
with any one person
for too long as some
kind of test of limited
solitude and its influences
or such—and I had a choice
of the person I'd take
with me to help me
make it or suffer
it through—it would
be her I'd choose.

She talks animals
through thunderstorms.
When you say you have
to go, she lets you.
She hears music in a
refrigerator's hum.

But, most of all,
I'd choose her
because she sees
ceilings in a corner.

Brother of Fifteen

My brother of fifteen,
Nudging into his own,
Wasn't good, wasn't mean.

An average haunted teen, he
(growing ever more bruised and alone)
stood shadowed by generations once fifteen.

In private wars against Mom and Dad's dreams,
He battled, shuffling their gold for his own
In streams of actions so sweetly mean.

Everything he screamed was "Me, me, me!"
On his shoulder rode a monkey of an ego
Grinding gestures typical of teens fifteen.

He'd not yet learned to spread imaginary wings
To lift himself to where Time had risen his soul;
So he remained momentarily grounded & miserably mean.

My brother of fragile and frantic fifteen
Needed only to ache, shiver, growl and grow.
He wasn't good; he wasn't mean;
He was just a brother of fifteen.

Master B

He is a builder.

When he comes all the
girls' heads are set
for *no,*
but he re-interprets
their language, fitting
it like everything else
into his own scheme of things.

He works on against
the hot sun:

long and slow,
the process he begins,
the gradual development
of a plan…the preparation,
and then the ground work—

> of sharpening points
> stringing them along
> making the final tie.

He works so hard
and long.
And when the work is done,
he is gone.

He is a builder,
and he knows his job well,
but he does not where he
lays ground dwell.

Daddy in Crimson Memory

Any bright red pick-up
truck with carpenter's racks
or ladders on the back

reminds me of when I was
a girl and my dad
drove my world.

Sometimes the rain
took from us everything
but sandwiches for lunch,

but his brown face,
cigarette stuck like
a thermometer, never

reflected defeat or got
as red as the truck even if
he'd had too many beers.

When I feel the heat
of the sun touch my arm
resting on the sill, I can

still feel memories
beaming crimson through
the pores of my skin

and I envision khakis
with a cuff and hands, big
and brown, but never rough,

and I see Dad holding the wheel
of a bright red truck and
balancing his arm on the

window sill. On hot sunny
carpenter's days, I remember
way back then when my dad worked

and I was a girl who
thought he ran the world.

Rock Change

Looking through
a bunch of old letters
of yours, Grandfather,
I see you weren't
always stuck rocking
on the front porch.

While dust touches not
your favorite chair,
it gathers round
what was once more important
to you than anything else.

Full of imagery and rhyme,
I found letter form a time
you were once in love.

Knocking the cobwebs away,
I thought of you of today,
as I met the man covered by dust.

I am glad to know
your weren't always
like some great gray owl;

you were once a nightingale.

Heavy Weights

Pumping, pumping, pumping
himself up; flattening,
toning, tanning and more;
making himself
empty and tough.

Routine, abstain,
gain, lose, refrain:

his life is made-up
of endless heavy weights.

He sweats,
pounds himself and it,
drills and drills
with every breath.

It takes all he has,
more than his
every last breath—

to pump and blow himself up.

I'll Call Hal Licked

"Got-damn!…What 'cha mean?
I- I- I-…hadn't had hard-ly
Uh…a…drink!"

a deep chill
confession builds strong, hard walls
                    pity piled on love

"Damn! Shit! I- I- I- said 'sit'
sit down right—right here…"

red eyes plead
innocent lies bleed emptiness
                    into experience

"Now I'm tellin' ya I hadn't had
hardly anything ta- ta- ah- drink."

eclipses earthy
groans from a large red hot moon
                    tears orbit moans

"Aw, now, Baby, don't cry…I- I'm
sorry…shush…so sorry."

ice warmed
by breath liquefies…melts…flames
                    in eyes, lies and blame

"Damn—woman—stop that now! Don't cry,
I'm home and I'm not drunk no-how!

a stranger
strangles family, friends and him, floods
                in revenge against guilt

"Hell! That's why I don't wanna come here!
I can't stand that whine-in!"

staggers out silence
stupor and regret, shivers something left
                just before its death.

E. E. Uh-ly Excited Are We

dedicated to the magic of e. e. cummings

everyone doesn't and everyone does
(with little inbetweens life & love)
beginning middle end and after
think on the perchance disaster

old and young (in hues of dawn)
fear paths not they're on
they smile frowns, forget names
stop go yield abstain in same

babes cry (in love's arms doomed)
they seem to know what comes too
after beginning middle and end
where everyone's alone when then

after the was and to step-to-foot
down we start, couldn't we could
yes by no and maybe no by yes
all to them is zero's best

everyones carry their everythings
their do-didn'ts and inbetween dreams
was he she (sun summer fun in fall)
scrape knees and sunburn all

abstain go yield stop
to be motion for the still stop
someones pull the strings to spin
with whirls another still go-round

a minute everyone lives i guess
(and less than that) we die i bet
hurried lives ignore seek-to-hide
inside outside helloes good-byes

now by now and then by then and
when by when we straighten to bend
everyone and no one life by winter
feel the shiver give and deliver

Old and young (in laughter and yawn)
feel the seasons of touches pass on
keeping their ifs creating whens
to stop go slow and begin again

Nepenthe

Raven, the night,
and so her dark flowing
hair—so where's the prince
promised here?

She swears,
she won't be a fair-haired
princess's joke—

Aladdin had his lamp,
Ali Baba his "open"-stroke;
where poetry, fairy-tales
and imagination abide,
lives aways a rewrite.

Scenario written
by girls sittin' on
shelves: up comes a knight,
(that's right—in bright & shining...)
down he jumps, then clanks on by.

One-thousand-and-one-tales
told of raven-haired beauties
passed when bright yellow stars
catch eyes is being revised.

Dark is the night;
waving arms like a bird in flight,
is a girl with flowing
raven-hair and a "Nevermore" stare.

DEAD-END: NO OUTLET

Sont

Maze: Man-Made

In laborious exertion
the animal attempted
to escape the labyrinth.

The maze's purpose:
to lacerate and
fulfill in all.

Sympathy is due
this creature who
refused to lament;

this one who would
not relent,
who worked

through tangled
complexity to an
unsatisfying end.

Emotions Between Mts.

My laughter
is only an echo
of the scream
you voiced
through me;

chasms of emotion
erupt so suddenly.

How treacherous can
be that space between
where we begin and
end——eventually.

Cavernous and hollow
are shells of love
washed apart,
but empty doesn't
begin to express
the sensation felt
when mountains
are moved.

In Pace Requiescat

When love dies,
it dies stone,
cold dead. And
you wonder,
"How did I ever
love that man?"

And you can't
imagine feeling
a chill at his touch
and nothing he says
grabs your guts or
hurts at all. It's
just like walking
over a puddle of mud:

You think to yourself
when you're on dry
solid ground again—
"Damn, I'm glad
I didn't fall in!"

Dry Kimberly

Because she is
our friend, we must
go in. Inside the labeled
door, she is propped-up
watching the hinge.

She pulls her
milk-stained robe across
her breast. We feel her cringe.

"Have you seen my baby?"

Trying to ignore tears
beginning to leak from her
face like water from a cracked,
leaking glass—

we smile, nod, stutter
and then make an excuse

to quickly go without allowing
the flowers or ourselves
to drink of the irrigation below.

In Need of Artemis or Arrows' Touch

They starve themselves,
these fragile
five-foot-seven
size three's.

Everyday is their
last slow fast.

They await, anticipate,
that ceremony at the table
and hate it when the last
person leaves the ladies'
room where there is room
for these celery sticks
of women to submit to
the crunch.

What a terrible thing
it must be to see
everything in life
coming up before you
in ripples you flush.

R. E. Tabler

Boy threw a rock
through the window,
owed a carwash and a lawn mow
      to gripey R. E.

Grocer bet the Mets would win,
a close friend borrowed fifty
and I a quarter from
      old R. E.

Now all are debt free 'cause last night
R. E. Tabler ceased
      to be.

The Cause and Course of Revolutions

Societal conceit:
open the door
and get out
of the way.

No. We don't
have anything
new to say;
nothing better
to replace what
we take.

Open the door
and get out
of the way.

Move. We
just want to
get thru.

A Wish at the Fountain of Fools

I hope I live long enough
    for people to be happy
    when I die;

For them to be tired
    of hearing my stories
    and weary of my smile.

I hope that when I go
    I am royally, eternally,
    ethereally thought crude

And that people yawn
    and resume their lives
    glad that I am through.

POET'S COVE

Sont

Some Things

Some things can only
live in poetry and are
in other genres like fish
out of water gulping
for a place to survive.

Some things can only
live on small bits of
print like parasites
on drops of blood.

Some things must be
free of the action
we cage on screens.

Some things must be
of what we feel:

of dew not rain,
of pain not tears,
of drought not desert,
of smiles not laughter

Some things must
be of poetry.

Falling for Poetry

Poetry is as
simple as pain.

The innocent
don't learn
a thing when
they reach for
that cerebral
terrain and
get burned.

Like little kids,
we love fire.

Is that all we
love—the desire?

Writing Poetry

if it rhymes, that's fine;
if it skips and hops, alliterates
or not, if it leaves spaces
or invisible question marks,
that's okay, too, because
all it has to be is you

whether you write, type it,
sing it, dream it, or CRT it
matters not, for like my dad used
to say: "if you're a poet, you'll
know it"
                    …but if it stays
in the hidden recesses filling
blanks, if it begins and never grows
or seeps out and doesn't shout
or make you smile; if you begin
and never seem to end, or if the balls
of paper you chunk aside match
the lumps in your stomach.

interpret this:

put the pen to the paper
like glue; poetry is not a voice for you

From Solitude: The Artist's Cry

Seagulls soaring overhead
remind me of where I am.
I stand at coasts where
they do feed.

Creeping to the water's
edge, I dip my feet.
Returning them to solid
ground, I fondle a fossil
washed to white sand and
roll it with my feet.

The living thing that
was once like me, that
once did fear the gulls
and sea is now a shell
I study at my feet,
                        I feed.

The ocean is lovely
and deep. It beckons
me.

Hemingway herald me not
that far along. Plath,
Roethke sing to me not
your sad songs:

if I come to like my
own lonely voice, let
me not be lost in shrill
tunes; let me at least
be like Emily and stay
in touch with white
touching only stars as asterisks
on pages where notes are rung.

Let me not be a Siren to myself.

The Hoarse Voice

I talk to myself;
I sit in rooms alone,
without music or anything else,
and I sing songs to myself—strange
songs—songs that play themselves.

Foddering in fabricated fogs,
adding thoughts upon thoughts
like to a fire—firelogs, I
stare at white ashen pages
and sometimes blow on them
until dawn.

        Sometimes I fall
asleep humming last words to
some poem, and I leak ink all
over the carpet like some
bleeding thing, wounded, and
needing to be put to sleep.

I curse a hoarseness
I notice in my voice
and move to the bed
where I start again.

Either I have something
to say,
or I'm just plain vain.

Either way—artist or insane—I
love the nothing, the pioneering
plight of searching through the night
and filling pages of white.

I want to be a ghost
that haunts library shelves.

ABOUT THE AUTHOR

Born in Dallas, Texas, in 1950, Sondra Tyler, who uses the pseudonym Sont, graduated from the University of North Texas, where she later received her Master's degree. She is presently an instructor of Literature and Composition at Eastfield College and Spruce High School. Her poems have appeared in numerous anthologies and poetry journals including: The *Anthology of New American Poets, The American Poetry Review, The Cambridge Collection of Treasured Modern Poets, Galaxy of Verse, Southern Review* and *Xandadu.*

www.ingramcontent.com/pod-product-compliance
Lightning Source LLC
Chambersburg PA
CBHW030352290526
45785CB00004B/1718